Copyright © 2020 Melissa & Matthew Pisani.

ALL RIGHTS RESERVED. This book contains material protected under International and Federal Copyright Laws and Treaties. Any unauthorized reprint or use of this material is prohibited. No part of this book may be reproduced or transmitted in any form or by any means, electronic or mechanical, including photocopying, recording, or by any information storage and retrieval system without express written permission from the author/publisher.

This is a work of fiction. Names, characters, businesses, places, events, and incidents either are the products of the author's imagination or used in a fictitious manner. Any resemblance to actual persons, living or dead, or actual events is purely coincidental.

ISBN: 978-1-64184-439-0 (Hardcover)
ISBN: 978-1-64184-440-6 (Paperback)
ISBN: 978-1-64184-441-3 (eBook)

Dedicated To

Mercy and Malakai

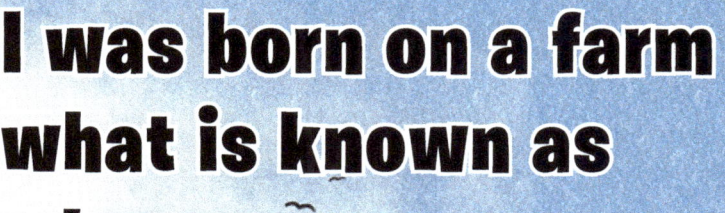

I was born on a farm what is known as a barn.

I have brown and white spots with a pink button nose.

My ears are floppy and I have webbed toes.

I hope that I will someday grow into my paws.

Just give me a rope and I'll start to pull.

I am strong and I am tough.

I am Nala the Bull!

I embrace how I'm made with all of my heart.

I love who I am, it's what sets me apart.

My life has a purpose, there's a reason I'm here!

NALA

Let's embrace our differences and spread some more cheer!

ABOUT THE AUTHORS

Matt and Melissa are parents, motivational speakers, and entrepreneurs. They have a non profit and podcast to encourage, bring hope and unity to their audience. They have a heart for people to know that their life has worth and purpose. Every child is fearfully and wonderfully made and is a gift from above.

For more information visit www.cleanslateliving.org
Podcast : The Puzzle is Real
Social Media:
@cleanslateliving
@puzzleisreal

ABOUT NALA

Nala loves walks on the beach, laying in the sun, and tug of war. She is sweet, loving, and a fierce protector. She is a French/English Bulldog and brings joy to everyone she meets.

www.ingramcontent.com/pod-product-compliance
Lightning Source LLC
Chambersburg PA
CBHW042033100526
44587CB00029B/4403